# A Tale of A Refugee

Gamar Abdulrahim

First published in Great Britain in 2021

Copyright © Gamar Abdulrahim

The moral right of this author has been asserted.

All rights reserved.

No part of this publication may be reproduced, stored in a retrieval system, or transmitted, in any form or by any means, without the prior permission in writing of the publisher, nor be otherwise circulated in any form of binding or cover other than that in which it is published and without a similar condition including this condition being imposed on the subsequent purchaser.

Editing, typesetting and publishing by UK Book Publishing

www.ukbookpublishing.com

ISBN: 978-1-914195-32-7

TO
MY FAMILY AND FRIENDS
WITH
LOVE AND RESPECT

*"I left my home for a reason; security and dignity are worth it"*

# Chapter One

All my life I had a dream which is to travel around the world exploring it, from London to Paris, Rome to New York, to see how these cities act upon life day and night. Even to discover the political issues that had so captivated me since I was a teenager.

Travelling is the one major task that a diplomat may encounter in his or her career in building a feasible relationship between countries. Being a diplomat requires a lot of knowledge, being a decisive figure.

It was 2002 when I come back from Darfur to find there was an advertisement for third secretary in the Ministry of Foreign Affairs, so I went to Kassala to take my certificate; Kassala is a beautiful city in the Eastern Sudan.

I went there overwhelmed with joy because I knew I would pass the exam no matter how tough it might be. I have the confidence and belief in my skills and my performance to be qualified as a successful diplomat. Nights in Kassala have a special flavour, cafés by the mountain, it's such an enchanting place to be in the wintertime, the weather is temperate, neither too hot nor too cold. I clasped my certificate and I went towards Khartoum full of confidence and hope.

In the bus I saw Lima, Paris and Brussels but those

destinations were just a dream, so I discounted them to accept the harsh truth that I had, in fact, arrived in Khartoum.

There in the office I found a young man. I asked him about the advertisement and he told me that it was the last day – "Would like to add your name on?" What a question! This was my dream. Then he asked about my certificate and I handed him everything in one big file.

After he finished registering me he wished me luck and I left. After five months the list was published. I found myself among nine thousand students; in such competition the number was massive, but I knew that I would be in the shortlist. I sat the exam, the three hour exam that could be the start of a brighter future.

I had waited for two months and then in the news I read that there might be a delay on the results which made me a little frustrated. I used to wait under a big tree when the secondary school asked me to help them because they were finding it hard recruit teachers and wanted me to help fill that gap whilst I was awaiting the result of my interview. So, I went into that job and gradually I managed the position. A year later the results were finally published and only 113 students had succeeded and I was number 45. The city lights shone upon my eyes and accompanied me even in my behaviour to cope with the new dream destination. I can't express how proud I was when I had my interview and I had met Altayib who reassured me by saying, "you belong here, man, so don't worry.'

The mobile rang, I saw it was Altayib's number. I answered and the joy was obvious in his voice. "Hey the results were posted on the internet but unfortunately your name wasn't listed." I was so shocked. I asked about him and he said, "Yes , for sure." I wished him all the best. I congratulated him many times and then the line went dead. Everything changed in an instant.

I stayed up that night regretting those hopes and dreams that had expired in front of me. It was the most unforgettable shock that I have ever had in my life.

I travelled back to Darfur, where I belong.

In the village many activities take place related to the common interest, mainly social events like weddings, deaths or funerals. Usually the villagers prepare a meal to be shared with the relatives of the dead individual and show some sympathy. Also, circumcisions with the lovely customs stuff from the village to be stolen and when the people want them back they should pay a piece of money to the circumcised boy or girl. In addition, the Naffeer, which includes any work done voluntarily for other weak individuals, whether building a new hut or a room for a newly married couple to start their new life, cultivate land for the growing season and looking for lost cattle and herds. I usually took part in every event because I believe it is my commitment towards my own people.

The electricity in Sudan varies from one area to another, the closer you are to the capital Khartoum, the better, and the further you go from the capital, you might find only a big generator which only lasts for five to six hours. Other villages are without any source of power for much of the time and a bulb is a miracle for them. The people always go to bed early in order to get in a great amount of sleeping, to be ready for the next day which they normally spent it in the hotter days and sometimes it is not predictable for the social activities; however, they are ready to participate in any events regardless of their business. In 2001 when the Twin Towers in New York were brought down, maybe the whole world saw it live while I only knew about it three days later by accident through the BBC radio. For most Sudanese the BBC has the highest credibility and is most trusted, and even they make a competition about the most accurate watch, that stroke at the same time with Big Ben.

I have two activities that I consider my hobbies, which differs from most of the people in my area: reading and spending time at the nearest Hafeer which is the secret place for lovers and those who smoke weed. Haffeer is a wide area designated to contain rainwater by excavating the land and is used as a reservoir in the time of drought and it is used as a source of water for animals and people. Many villagers suffered disease like malnutrition and bilharzia from the dirty water.

On moonlit nights I enjoyed myself, whether by singing or contemplating the welfare of citizens or imagining the eyes of my true love, the surface of the moon sparkling and reflecting on the surface of water. In the daytime my friends and I, in our spare time, we played throwing stones or what is called Stone Skipping, over the surface of Haffeer water and the winner was the one who scored as many touches of the stone on the water. I came second to Osman who was master of the game. I was fascinated by the tranquillity of my area and the peace covering the humble houses and faces of the people. In my opinion living away from this friendly environment is like a suicide, as if the roots of a tree had been pulled out of the fertilized soil; therefore I never thought I'd be away from there, no matter how hard the circumstances.

Now I still feel the homesickness to be there, five thousand miles away. I still miss the laughter and joyful time when they speak about the football league standings, amongst the rivalry between Hilal and Marreikh whom I support – this usually takes place in the dusk or even in any gathering of people. Football is a passion for most of them regardless of the performance of both teams.

One day during a midterm holiday I was sitting with my friends when the headmaster shouted at me. When I approached him he saluted me 'Oh Teacher'. I said hi then he told me that our English teacher was on sick leave "and you are here doing nothing, therefore, instead of that you can help your own community through teaching the secondary school classes until the return of the teacher". I answered, "It would be my honour to work with you and leave a mark on the coming generation," and I said, "I will come tomorrow to see how to help and take a tour of the school and familiarize myself with the schedule." But he insisted that "you are going to come with me right now".

At the school I managed to do many things, especially for the remedial classes for those who are below level. The school has six classes, three for the boys and three for the girls surrounded by lovely trees and some water pots under the shade.

It was built on the edge of the village through a local committee, I mean their own money for the sake of the future of the children. In other areas the classes are mixed gender for the few numbers of students. The students are between 13 and 15 years old. I did a lot of hard work with the school until I become the deputy headmaster. Then in 2013 there was a protest against the government's policy of rising costs of petrol and all sectors of the students took part in the protest. One of my students was shot dead by the police and while we were attending the funeral and every individual was condemning the act of killing innocent young people, a pickup car approached the graveyard and started to capture those who were at the protest and I was among them. I spent twenty-four days in detention and when I was released I found myself jobless due to the absence without permission. I tried to speak to the headmaster but in vain; he asked me to provide any evidence of being detained in NISS "and I will let you commence your work immediately".

So I went to the NISS to ask for any proof but they refused – unless you cooperated with them and gave them any information about the movements and their leaders' detailed steps and write a report about the activists who were keen to make trouble for the government... They told me I was being monitored, every step, just like my shadow. I suffered paranoia and I felt I was not safe anymore; therefore I decided to flee the country.

# Chapter Two

## DARFUR, THE BLEEDING REGION

On 2nd of September 2001 I headed towards Darfur to complete my compulsory service as a teacher. The train left Khartoum station at 9 in the morning. A lot of people were there to say farewell to their relatives and wish them a safe journey. Only my brother Saif was there for me, as if I was no longer important to others, therefore, I no longer had fear. We passed many cities and villages, some of them extraordinary, beside the Nile or white Nile till we arrived at Nayala, the capital of southern Darfur. Believe or not it took me five days to reach there; my colleague and I used to sleep on the iron floor of the train because we were exhausted. This brings into focus the negligence of the region from the basic infrastructure, scarcity of teachers, doctors and even theme parks, regardless of the components of the multi environmental area.

In Nayala I met many people from many parts of Sudan, or you can say it was a small Sudan, as it seemed to me. In the market I saw many new issues – the chicken and meat can be served on the street not like a restaurant, or you can have a small shelter for that; the price was astonishing compared with the price in Khartoum. Young girls worked as builders on a very hot day. I spent a week waiting for the dispersal among the schools of Nayala. It was ironic that the famous accidents worldwide were seen live through the news stations or TV whereas I heard it on 13 September when I listened to the radio that there had been an attack on the commercial centre in the USA. Later, that week I was sent back to Aldeian, another city south-east of Nayala. I had to wait a whole month for the students to come to school because they were busy with their families harvesting the crops – they grow wheat, melt and Dura. Most of the Darfurian were farmers and herdsmen in the place where I worked; the Omadah had more than five thousand cattle – when they were on the move it took approximately half an hour to reach the end of the line.

For women in a society where the men dominated, like other Middle Eastern countries, I saw that when a woman had to speak to a man in her society she should kneel down to speak as sign of respect. Meanwhile, my colleagues and I were invited almost by the whole community, they were so generous and they would feel disgrace if you turned down their invitation. We participated in such an occasion, a wedding where we danced and (Hakama) a woman singer sang for us.

Even in( Jawdeya) to make agreement between two group of people who had a dispute, we had seen many obstacles had been solved by the local authority like sheikhs or Omadas. Strangely, they were agreed upon and no one could act awkwardly after the (Jowdeya) meeting is over.

Mara Mountain is the most outstanding place to visit so at the end of the school year we arranged a trip to Mara. The view was spectacular: meadows, springs of water, waterfalls and wild animals. You wouldn't believe it unless you saw it with your own eyes. I know now it is not safe to visit it because you might be killed; however, the scenery is fabulous. I hate War, I hate it. Thousands of innocents were killed in this war, which broke out just a year after I returned back to Khartoum and lasted for fifteen years. The results were catastrophic for both human beings and the land, even Mara Mountain which can be a tourist attraction for people looking for relaxation and sightseeing.

# Chapter Three

*"A man can be destroyed, but not defeated"*
Ernest Hemingway

SUDAN
APRIL 2016
2:15 P.M.

In a tyrant's regime as in many African countries, to have political views against the government, you are considered to be the ultimate and open enemy for them; the government will accuse you of treason and position. In a treason trial there is neither defence nor evidence against their horrible allegations. Three different experiences with the National security who always the treat the citizen as a slave and beat them to death. You can regard yourself lucky if you are released alive.

On Friday 4th of January 2016 we were having a meeting in our school when the National Security members interrupted the meeting and took us all away – me and my friend who were the teachers – they accused us of preparing strategies to collect money and more information to give to the rebel movements. After twenty-four days they set me free on certain conditions. I went to the school to recommence my career as usual but I was told by the headmaster that I had been dismissed by the secondary level authority, so I no longer belonged there, "so please leave and if you have any questions just go to them". What!

This was my first time in Souq Libya, the weather was so hot like Sudan's summer days. I thought Souq Libya was totally precarious and eccentric. Many different faces I came across. I passed many shops then I reached what I was looking for: (The White Rose) it wasn't white, only the colour on the paint. The shop is designated to sell clothes and some plastic furniture such as chairs, tables and armchairs, different shapes and colours. After a while I could recognize that the work was in hard currency, I mean buying and selling Dollarsand Euros.

"Sayed" was the name of the agent whom I should meet. The person in the shop was in his early twenties so I doubted that would be him. He welcomed me, thinking that I was a customer and I said, "I'm looking for Sayed." He said, smiling, "You've reached your destination."

He ordered the lad who worked with him as an assistant to run to the nearest supermarket to bring me a soft drink, then he looked at me and said, "Which one you prefer, bottled or fresh?" He recommend the latter and I nodded as a sign of agreement. Actually in such hot weather you have no choice but to drink as much beverage as you can. I sweat very heavily over my whole body, the shirt appeared as if it was wet and you wear it. I waited for an hour, many people came to buy, the salesperson had an attractive smile and catchy words to persuade customers to take a close look at his goods and teasing them – "if you went back home you will regret not buying from me" – amazingly everyone who stepped into the shop would never leave without buying. I asked him jokingly, "Are you a magician?" He laughed and said, "No, but you know this is persuasion and it is one of the attributes you should have in such occupations."

I drank the juice and by the last sip of it somebody stopped in front of me. "SALAM" in a very strong bass voice; he was tall, wearing casual dress. "Are you Ali?" I answered, "yes". He nodded OK. He approached the salesperson and he whispered in his ear then he told me to follow him but not so close – "there should be twenty metres gap; is that understood?" I nodded.

I followed him as he advised me; however, the paths were crowded so I had to focus in order not to miss him in the crowd. I had a backpack with some dates, a torch and two shirts and Panadol tablets so that when I felt tired from the heat I could take one or two. He stopped and waited till I came close to him and he spoke to me: "You see that land cruiser, over there?" I said, "Yeah."

"Just go and ride, they are waiting for you, I hope you reach Libya safe, the pursuit for settlement and equality."

No time to say thank you, I looked towards the vehicle and he disappeared between the crowds. I approached the SUV car and the door opened for me then started moving at once. I was so pleased because the vehicle was air conditioned and I felt relieved. After an hour the vehicle stopped and there was another car waiting for us. So, the human trafficking process never takes just one route in its progress, I mean they handled groups of people after groups of people. There were eleven passengers when I arrived the vehicle plus six who had come in the SUV car. Ahmed was funny, I liked him, he kept saying "take it easy" even in dangerous situations; sometimes it worked. The driver stated some conditions and rules to be blindly followed otherwise you could face death in the middle of the desert. I listened tentatively and many images crossed my minds, my parents, the voice of my mother everyday preparing the morning tea, my father and his lovely lively laugh, my twins playing beside me, my wife's words goodbye as she kissed me farewell, full of tears, I promised her I'll be OK and soon we can get together in Europe, or if I didn't make it, forgive me. Her eyes brimmed with tears. I tried hard to extract myself and let her go, it was the weakest moment that I have ever had in my life. The twilight made a colourful picture upon the horizon. When the driver commenced his journey he drove at high speed as if he was being chased or in a rally. I had to hold on tight to the side of the car. He did a tremendous drive, he didn't take care, high hills or low lands. I was thrilled about that; I kept saying farewell to the remaining scatter of houses, I knew that it would be the last view of civilization I would see. The machine roared in the air and all of a sudden we dived into the vast open desert towards darkness and an unknown destiny. I felt as If I was sinking in a deep ocean of worries.

# Chapter Four

*"The cure for anything is Salt water,
sweat, tears or the sea"*
Isaak Dinesen

SOMEWHERE IN THE SAHARA

From time to time the driver stopped to refuel the car, give us some water and allow us to pass water and stretch our limbs. The amount of water designated for a person was a teacup three times a day, so you could barely feel it through your throat. The faces were weak and tired. Lips were cracked, stinky mouths and a high level of dehydration. Therefore, when you feel the desire to pass water it may take up to fifteen minutes to do so.

In the desert you feel a bad need to pee but you can't do it, so you might wait for two to three minutes to pass water. After the first three nights had passed, the worries passed and soon death is no longer a terrifying matter. However, the next day the driver stopped for a vacant or deserted car to check what was going on with them. Everything was still and suddenly he yelled, "Oh, My God!" Not ten metres from the car: four dead bodies. He said they had died two days ago, due to shortage of water and fuel. The bodies were starting to dissolve, their features were changed. I checked my passport so I could be easily recognized among the dead. We buried them and the driver took advantage of their stuff and two tyres for himself and restarted the journey. I asked the driver, "How many days remain?"

"It depends, maybe five or six, don't panic, we will make it, please GOD "inshallah".".

On the tenth day we arrived at small village in Libya. There we met the asset who took us to his boss "Jabber". He treated us badly as if we were slaves, queue us then started cursing at us using taboo words. After counting us he forced us into a big truck with many other different nationalities, different religious beliefs. We were seventy passengers in a small tiny truck. They spoke very fast. I could hardly grasp some Arabic words; they were armed and drunk. The truck took two hours to reach Sabha.

They put all of us in a big farm, they forced us to work on the farm and if you wouldn't work you had to redeem your soul which was more than two thousand dollars. Two Somalis refused to work – they gave them one week to receive the money. One day the man came in in a hurry. "Where is my fucking money?"

"We don't have money," one of the Somalis answered.

"So I'm going to kill you, shit! You are nothing but a slave so you can't say No to me."

Then he took a big knife. I was trembling – is he seriously going to kill them, slaughtering them? Two men came to hold one and the man with the knife cut one of his ears off in cold blood. The Somali cried in agony. "You will be an example for the others," then he shouted: "This will be your fate if you don't comply with orders."

# Chapter Five

After the scene of the chopped ears on the ground Ahmed told me we should run for our lives, as if we stayed here we might face the same end or even worse. It should be at night when the guards were drunk and had taken one of the girls to be raped. Others had been beaten to death or had to pay a ransom through videotaping them to send to their relatives to see how they were tortured and could help them out of this hell.

At 3 o'clock Ahmed woke me up and we sneaked out and jumped over the wall and ran for good. No specific place or direction, but to run as fast as we could. When the sun rose we saw an old man working on his farm. We greeted him and we asked for the directions to Tripoli. He said he could give us a ride if we gave him 200 dollars. We agreed and by the time the sun went down we had arrived in the city. I met some friends there and later reached "Jabber". He welcomed us both and the same night we went to Sabratha. A big warehouse full of people, maybe 400, and there we stayed for twenty-eight days. A slice of bread and cheese for breakfast and for dinner. Ahmed bought some dates from the market which we shared. We had been told that the police were patrolling the coast, so they had to wait until they found the right time to send the people to the sea, at night. We had been chosen among the people whom they took to the boat at 3 o'clock in the morning. I was absolutely terrified because the trip before ours, all the passengers drowned in the sea. The Mediterranean Sea is a total graveyard where thousands of people lie there. I was happy to meet Ahmed there; actually he was upset when they didn't choose him but fortunately one of the selected people was terribly ill so they chose Ahmed instead.

In a small balloon boat we managed and I tried to help others to reach the boat. I moved till the water reached up to my waist. Girls, women and children: we were 120 individuals. We started the journey, this time towards the sea and the high waves and many images came into my mind. Ahmed was scared, he recited the Quran all the way, not only Ahmed but everyone started to pray in his language; we shared the same hope to be safe "ALLAH". I knew if I could survive this I could survive anything else in life. After three hours of sailing, the engine broke down.

"It was a dead body," the one in charge explained why the boat had stopped. "So I need some help and please calm down because if you keep moving perhaps we will all sink." He tried to start the engine over and over.

One of the group jumped into the water to check what was going on with the engine peddles. He found that some of the clothes were stuck on them. Moreover, he asked the man to start the engine then suddenly there was a scream. I looked over my shoulder and I saw many dead bodies, or to be more precise, the remains of bodies due to attacks by sharks and other sea creatures. Ahmed burst into tears. "Ali, we are going to die like them."

"No, I don't want to die here," I told him. "You, Ahmed, don't panic, stay still, otherwise we are going to have the same destiny."

Then all the passengers were silent, only weeping and humming could be heard. After an hour the captain checked the engine and after two goes it started and faces sparkled with joy and relief, but the person who was in the water had lost two of his fingers when he tried to clean the peddle. I gave him my T-shirt to bandage the wound. We came close to a huge ship, a commercial one, and the captain tried to avoid them because they made a big current and wave. Then a grey helicopter flew over our heads and came so near and we yelled "HELP, HELP". Then it disappeared. Then after one hour a small boat approached our boat so the captain switched off the engine and asked the people to stay calm. The boat was the police – it had written on the side "POLICIA". They asked the captain, "How many are you?" He shouted, "125 persons."

"Where have you come from?"

"Libya."

So while the interrogation took place another four boats came close – Red Cross, Army and governmental agencies.

They took the injured man first who had lost so much blood, they wore a white apron with masks. Then they took the old and families, I mean women and children. We were so lucky to be rescued by the Italian navy; we abandoned the small boat and felt safe in the huge ship with stuff like life support equipment.

I can't express my feeling when I found myself safe and secure after the long journey from Sudan and through the desert and the Libyan savages, through the deadly sea where the smell of death spread all over. I hoped at that moment that I were Mel Gibson so that I could picture these images and feelings into a great movie and amazing soundtrack behind those scenes.

# Chapter Six

SUDAN
SOMEWHERE IN DARFUR

My wife counted the days and nights and every time assured her son that "your father will soon be settled and we all be united again". The baby boy continued crying, ignoring these empty words – all he needed was his father's touches and cuddling, his voice which cheered him up and kept him smiling.

Morning tea is always a new starting day program, Yousef was still in his cradle surrounded by many clothes and the sponge used as diapers; beside him a shirt of his father to comfort him when he cried – his mother believes that with the smell of his father's sweat he would become calm and smile.

She usually fed Yousef and went to collect wood for the fire to cook food for her and her ill mother who had broken her back after falling from a horse. Fatima had to walk for almost three miles in order to collect a pretty good amount of firewood that would satisfy her for a couple of days. She knew that Yousef was awakening through the milk from her breasts. When she reached the edge of the village she could hear his weeping and she walked as fast as she could and carrying the bunch of dry sticks and branches on her head with the part of her Thobe used as a turban in order to soften the hardness of the sticks upon her scalp. The sun started to slap faces with heat, therefore, her face was covered with sweat and appeared as if she had had a shower, her armpits were full of sweat and the dress stuck to her slim body. She had nothing to be clean for, for Ali wasn't there so she hadn't bothered to clean herself and shave her body or even to put on Hinah over her feet or hands. She put the sticks beside the hut where there was a designated area called (Tukul) small kitchen and started a fire. Sometimes the villagers mix the sticks with cattle's dung to keep the fire lasting a bit longer. After that she was breastfeeding Yousef and chatting with her mother.

"Love, please, after breakfast go and ask Alzabir the chemist if he knows any news about Ali."

"Mom, I went to him many times and all in vain."

"Baby, you have not to lose hope."

"Ok, I will."

From time to time she bought meat from the local market after she sold eggs and butter; breakfast was always porridge with yoghurt or weekah or smelly fish. The market opens early Wednesday morning every week and closes early evening, therefore, if you missed this you have to wait for the next week whether you want to sell or buy goods. For villagers, after breakfast there comes the coffee and usually tears come from Fatima's eyes when she remember Ali and his love for coffee, especially when she made it – he always commented "this is the most wonderful coffee that I have ever tasted. May Allah give you more strength and live longer."

"I feel he is OK and I could see that in my dreams he will be safe because I prayed very solemnly for God to keep him safe, fit and well. I suppose my God won't let me down." Fatima in her own soul could feel him assure her by saying 'Fatima, I am fine. I missed you so, so much, how are you? Yousef, your mother, everyone in the village.'

She woke up next morning full of joy and conveyed this dream to her mother. She always made sure that her mobile phone was fully charged and the signal was full, therefore, she went to the youth club, the only place where you can find electricity; however, you have to pay £5 to the man who she hates, because many times he asked her cunningly about Ali – "If you haven't received any news – don't waste your time waiting in vain, I can make you happy and look after your mother and your son," said Moawia.

Moawia was considered to be of the most successful businessmen in the village with many phenomenal ideas that seemed to be weird for villagers who were limited to the normal life; most of them are farmers and the others are shepherds. He got married twice and had about ten children.

"It's not your business and if you are the last man in the world I won't marry you, I wouldn't change Ali at all, even if I missed him forever I wouldn't marry another guy."

# Chapter Seven

ITALY
1ST JUNE 2016

"I'll never make this again, never," said Ahmed.
"Me neither, thank Allah we are safe."
There was a great pleasure on all faces and you could touch it. Red Cross took all the migrants to a big old school where we had a rest and got washed, they gave us clothes and food. After two days, the police came and distributed all the migrants into hostels and cheap hotels among the Italian cities.

The things I liked most about Italy: the weather, it was fine; building are old with historic views and decorated with fine arts; the gardens and benches everywhere. Ahmed and I were in the same room in Ancona. Ancona is a sea port northeast of Rome. It has small population. We were pleased to have the right to live like humans, treated with respect; the language is difficult but interpreters were there, even on call. It was a small town surrounded by hills and mountains, so quiet. While were in the city centre we met some Sudanese who had been there for two years. They weren't content with the situation there, and therefore said, "If you want to have a good life go to France." I asked him why. And he clarified many reasons which from my point of view seemed so logical. We had a little chat and then said bye and went back to the hostel. Eventually we decided to leave Italy and sneak into France.

The best way is by train and most convenient; however, despite the control a lucky few got to France.

Ahmed usually said, "This place is good so if you leave you might not find anything, even the breakfast, washing yourself, your clothes, dinner and a warm mattress to sleep on."

"But think what your purpose is?" I asked. "To be healthy, eat and sleep and that's it! No more?"

"What do you want to say?" asked Ahmed.

"I think it is better to move on and it is a good chance to see France, Paris where the fashion is, and at least you can speak French."

"So that's your idea! ..."

"Yes."

"Ok, let's get prepared for the adventure, but you know after these risky journeys I think once you find the safe place you definitely are going to settle here after we have been rescued by the Italian navy."

We travelled to Ventimiglia where we met many refugees from different nationalities. They took over one of the ancient churches as a hotel and shelter. Various organisations came to help; they provided food, clothes and blankets. We slept in sleeping bags rough on the street, when there was not sufficient food and our bodies were in bad need for food. Ahmed discovered a nearby McDonald's.

In the rubbish of the restaurant we found the meal that we had dreamt about when we were starving.

One day while we were on our night shift suddenly

it rained heavily and we got wet and soaking. We took a sidewalk to stay away from the rain. A lady approached us. "Hi!"

I replied, "Hi."

"My name is Franciscka, but you can call me Fran. What are your names?"

"I'm Ali and this is my friend, Ahmed."

She shook our hands and smiled, she was a typically pretty Italian lady with a hard English accent, and she had a piercing in her nose just like some Sudanese women.

"Where are you from?"

"Sudan."

"Why are sitting here?"

"To avoid the rain."

"Ok, my apartment is not far from here, just around the corner."

"Thank you."

Ahmed asked me what was going on with this lady and I told him that she had offered us a shelter to be dry and away from the rain.

"Come on, I know it is not that big but you can stay the night instead of this place in such a weather."

Ahmed liked the idea and I agreed.

"Ok. Let's go."

She was right, it was very small flat – when you opened the door there was a long corridor at the end of which was the kitchen.

"It's small but you are welcome," said Fran.

"It is just like heaven compared with where we were. Thank you for your kindness."

"Make yourself at home," she said earnestly. "Take your clothes off, don't feel shy!"

I said that in Arabic to Ahmed because he doesn't

understand English, only Yes, No, Thank you and Bye. Without warning Ahmed started taking his clothes off, down to his boxers. I saw her looking at him admirably and wetting her lips.

Ten minutes later, hot cups of tea and cakes were on the table.

"If you'd like more just ask me."

I told her most of the story and after we finished our tea, she said, "I think it is time to go to bed, so both of you go to sleep in my double bed."

I refused; we aren't going to leave her to sleep on the couch. "I will sleep in it you can sleep as usual." She agreed then she turned to say, "You know, I think Ahmed could sleep beside me in the double bed; it is big and can fit both of us." I told Ahmed about her suggestion and he agreed immediately saying "any place" and then she switched off the light.

Twenty minutes later I was soundly asleep.

The sea...

It was such a horrible experience so for weeks upon arrival in Italy whenever I went to sleep I had that nightmare or even the feeling of motion up and down with the waves or even dead bodies. I felt shaking and rumbling from side to side, even though the couch was comfortable and so I woke up in the middle of the night.

I could hear moaning voices from Fran's room. I thought that I was still sleeping. I opened my eyes wide and I saw a dim light and heard heavy breathing. "Is that REAL?"

"For God's Sake!"

Come on, Ahmed! I gently rose from the couch and went towards the room to understand exactly what was happening; I was right, I saw Fran totally naked on the top of Ahmed. I couldn't express my feelings!

I wondered was that the price she deserved, my fellow, to fuck her, it was so absurd. I went back to sleep, placing the pillow over my head to avoid listening to their voices of ecstasy.

At first Ahmed and Fran couldn't get along because of the language barrier; however, they found they could understand each other physically.

# Chapter Eight

The dream moved to me passing from one ordeal to another hardship. Previously, to come out miraculously from Sahara, then into the sea and its high waves which drown and send away unwanted poor souls to rest by the seashore or even be eaten by the sharks. To cross the border was a tremendous achievement that a migrant could fulfil during his life, seeking safety and security. I kept telling Ahmed while we were in Libya that when we arrive in Italy we will seek asylum there and we will feel the meaning of being human. Now, I told him to reach France and stay there. For many reasons and ambitions.

I thought it would be easy to cross the border like between Sudan and Libya. Actually, there were many things in common between Sudan-Libya border though, some race and language and some ethnic groups know the Sahara better than others; besides, the border is wide and open desert so it is difficult to be monitored by police.

I was dreaming about crossing the French border when someone whispered, "Hey, Ali, good morning." The smiling face of Fran was in front of me.

"Morning, Fran."

"Did you sleep well?"

"Yes, thank you for asking."

"You are welcome."

"We also had a great sleep, Ahmed taught me some Arabic words: 'Salam Alaikum'."

"That's great."

Then Ahmed came in exhausted and sat beside me. "Good morning."

I replied, "Good morning."

"You know I fucked her yesterday!"

"I know," I gesture. "You are so mean to take advantage of the sleeping lady who sheltered you and pay that favour by fucking her!"

"No, she started it, she told me if I can make a massage for you, then it finished in a different way."

"Ok, keep your voice down."

She was in the kitchen preparing the breakfast when she arrived. I said, "Thank you, Fran, for your support and your warm hospitality, you are an angel."

We ate the breakfast: boiled eggs, jam, cheese and some olives. She asked me about our plans and I told her that we were going to France. She wondered why: "If you stay here I will help you to resettle and integrate easily in the community."

I interpreted that for Ahmed who was so enthusiastic about staying in Italy and I could understand his reason. "I think France would be better than Italy." I saw Rome, Marseille and Ventimiglia but not in my dream scope of a diplomat.

"We are going to France, shall we, Ahmed?"

Before he could move Fran sat beside Ahmed and held his hand from the elbow and said, "Ahmed is not going with you."

"Ahmed, are you going to stay here?"

"No," said Ahmed.

"Ok. Let's go."

Then Fran asked me to wait. She went to her room and came running and gave me some money. I refused to take it but she insisted telling me that "you will need it on your journey to buy a train ticket to Nice and buy food and some drinks and even proper clothes, so if you buy clothes no one could recognize you on the train".

I thanked her for that then she guided us to the train station. We bought two tickets and got on the train to Nice. I told Ahmed we should not sit together to raise suspicions so each of us would be on a different carriage. The moments went slowly and the inspector came to check my ticket while I was chatting with a French old woman about my origin. She told me that her husband was from Senegal, she had met him in Paris when he was a student there. The inspector just punched my ticket and continued with his mission. I was so delighted to reach Nice.

# Chapter Nine

I still remember the feeling I felt when I was on the move in France – "unwanted" or blankly "you aren't welcome here". I could see that in their eyes as if you were a bug and they would have to squash you and get rid of you; but sometimes you can meet warm hearted people who help you with everything they can.

The streets are so clean and the areas are very quiet as if there is no one living there. There is romance wherever you go, a hug here and a kiss there, and a cuddle over there and even the old people walk hand in hand, feeling like they belong. My destination was to reach Paris or the city of light and fashion. I jumped on a train from Nice to Marseille. Luckily I reached Paris and this time without buying a ticket.

It was Ramadan when I arrived so it was difficult to do fasting while you have no option but to fast because you can't find any decent food, and then by the time of breaking fasting there were a lot of other temptations on the streets. Long hours of fasting could be up to eighteen hours, and by the time of breaking fasting many French people came to ELLE CHABEL, I mean under the bridge where I found many others sleeping rough on the street. I found Ashraf, a slim Sudanese young man, full of hope not far from Gare du Nord.

"Hello, as-salamu alaikum."

He answered, "When did you arrive here?"

"Two days ago and you?"

"Yesterday."

"What's your name?"

"Ashraf, and you?"

"Ali."

"How about the break fasting?"

"Don't worry, Ali, soon there will be good Muslim individuals who provide meals and refreshments for refugees. All we need to do is just be at the place."

"Where?" I asked.

"Here under the bridge."

"Ok it sounds good."

We shared everything even the cup of coffee and after one hour it was time for bed. "So, Ashraf, what are you going to do?"

"Just grab a carton over there and lie down here, that's it."

"Really!" Shocked.

"So when will we have an appropriate place to live, decent place I mean?"

"Only Allah knows."

I closed my eyes and fell asleep beside Ashraf in the street. I couldn't believe that I was in Paris, one of my dream cities to be visited – instead of formal meetings with VIPs I was sleeping in the street. Two hours later it started to rain heavily and I woke to find Ashraf smoking and thinking.

"I am cold, Ashraf!"

"Take this coat."

"Thank you."

"You know, we should go to Calais, they said that you can have your own tent, warm clothes and plenty of food."

"Where is Calais?"

"It's three hours from here by the train, it is a small city by the English Channel so it is easy; you can find a way to reach England."

"Great."

Next morning after many attempts we took the train to Boulogne then from there to Calais. I had left Paris without even walking in the Champs Elysees or seeing the Eiffel Tower and enjoying the view but maybe later and with a different perspective.

One of the socialist Parisians felt sympathy about my circumstances and he said that he would do anything to help me. I replied I just wanted help to speak to my family and without hesitation he handed me his mobile phone and I phoned my family in Sudan to let them know where I was. He spent some minutes and then he disappeared and after a while he had come back carrying a new mobile phone plus a credit voucher of €5 – I couldn't thank him enough for that gift.

# Chapter Ten

Since last June the last news about Ali when Alzabir the chemist heard people speaking about the terrifying experience in Libya had been conducted by savage militia and he told Fatima "someone had seen your husband among the detainees who have been treated as slaves". I haven't given up on my husband because my heart tells me he is OK and soon will come back. I had been thrown from worry to stress about my future – was it my bad luck to lose my kind father and my lovely husband together and no one left but graveness and loneliness.

Day after day I could see him beside me milking the cows, playing with Yousef, waving from the horizon – even at night I could clearly see him between the shining stars. I told Yousef don't be worried, soon we will meet your father here and there I could feel that, soon.

Fasting in Sudan is great challenge for people who live without a source of power and less infrastructure. The temperature could reach up to 48 degrees at midday although it sometimes comes during the rainy season. Nevertheless, those who live in such conditions, all they hope for is a cold place or an electric fan. Seriously, they have invented many ways through which they could cope with the heat of summer.

One Ramadan night while I was sleeping my mobile phone rang. I was so exhausted that I didn't move a limb but I just jumped and grabbed the mobile and answered:

"Hello."

"Hello."

"Who is this?" I asked.

"It's me, Ali."

I can't express my feelings, the tears of joy and bitterness mixed together and I couldn't find my voice.

"Hello, Fatima, are you still there?"

"Yes, I am here. How are you, sweetheart? Are you good?"

"Yes, I am and I miss you so, so much. How are you, Yousef and your mother? I hope you are all ok!"

"Yes we are. Where are you, darling?"

"I'm here in Paris."

"Where is Paris?"

Where is Paris? She wondered.

"It's in France."

"Then where is the so-called France?"

"Don't worry about that."

"Is it far from Libya?"

"Too far." Ali giggled into the phone.

"You know, I missed this laugh."

"I love you, Fatima."

"Me too, sweetheart."

Fatima felt relieved and as if a heavy weight had been moved away from her chest. Now I could sleep with empty worries and live longer for a purpose, to meet my love again. He told me about his dangerous journey and the lovely weather in France. Also, he declared his mortal love for me and his attention to cross the border to the UK. I begged him to stay there and no more risky adventure. The important thing was that he could apply for a family reunion so that we could live together happily ever after. He kept calling me from time to time up to Eid ul adha when suddenly he stopped calling or even texting me until one day he called me and said I made it, I am in the UK.

I could fly on the air and he asked me to make a big feast for the villagers and tell them Ali had achieved his goal and reached England safe and secure.

# Chapter Eleven

CALAIS to me was a gate of salvation. It is so quiet that sometimes you feel yourself in an abandoned city. The streets aren't as busy as a town. The roads are almost vacant except some elderly people or teenagers riding bicycles. I have never seen such a quiet area like that. We were five friends arriving at Calais, it was three o'clock, at the train station. I liked the music, SNCF, it was so awesome. With the announcements of course I could guess some of the words.

The path from the station to the refugee camp or that so-called "Jungle", is about half an hour on foot. I asked myself many times why did they called it jungle and there were three main possibilities for that: it was a jungle, in fact; and it was a place where apes live; and sometimes it's racial discrimination.

I was so excited to see the camp; however, unfortunately I felt shocked for what it was. It was a primitive area with randomly scattered tents here and there; some of the inhabitants queued to get some stuff, hygiene, another queue for the water. It was drizzling so when we reached there we were so soaked, so we just needed a place where we could change our clothes. I asked one of the Sudanese where we could find a place and he told me if you are new wait till tomorrow at 9 o'clock in the morning so you can get a new tent, mattress and a blanket. He guided us to the Sudanese tent, a very big modern plastic tent.

Calais is not a good place to be remembered, a place where drugs and sex were prevalent which affected the young people. No existence of law, I mean no presence of police, just by the edge of the camp, so the wild legislation may be applied.

There were some Englishmen in the Sudanese tent who worked to build up the tent, I mean re-erect it – it had been demolished and burnt in the last clashes between Sudanese and Afghanis, even the woman who came to help the whole group had been threatened with being killed, but she wouldn't stop, she is a brave woman. The conflict lasted for two days according to the witness, many died, many injured, badly injured – one lost one of his eyes, another paralysed and stayed months at the hospital neglected from the people.

Mahjoob, a Sudanese man, told me the whole story, bitterly, but sometimes hilarious and funny. A tall man ran for his life when the crisis was over, they came to talk about courage and bravery and how they might defend the tent and fight back.

I have a question in mind. Where were the police when the fight started?

"The police came in the camp but not to settle the situation."

"For what?"

"To ensure that the facilities of the Al salaam Camp are safe."

Their concern was for the facilities not the human

beingd so they never acted upon the fight at all; that's so disgusting!

When night falls the refugees get out just like rats in the jungle to catch a lorry or any vehicle to cross the border, so if you want to cross the border to the UK you should try hard or you will stay here forever.

Doghar is a blockage made by refugees to stop the motorway trucks and lorries where others who were lucky and fast get into the lorries, some could make it through, some others keep trying.

The first time for me, it was two o'clock at night when I saw a stranger pull a truck and branches to close the way. Ten minutes later a very fast lorry crashed into the trunk and then a small car slightly diverted from the way and crashed into the barrier then fire burst out. I tried to run when I saw the police siren and lights above the sign. The migrants ran towards the lorries to get in and suddenly I heard "HELP"… "help me please!" I ran towards the sound and I found the driver was bleeding, his face was all bloody. I unfastened the seat belt and pulled him out; his leg was broken. I told him to stay calm, police will soon arrive. He thanked me and wished me a safe crossing. "You have saved my life" – and I said to him, "you make my day." When the police were on the highway I threw a stone at them so they would come after me to help this man. I ran as fast as I could and disappeared into the wood. They spoke French so I couldn't understand them but anyway I was thrilled because I had saved a man's life.

In Calais the atmosphere was unpredictable, quite like the whole town or noisy and fun like 14th July night at the beach. You might wake up to hear two migrants had been raped, another robbed, three made their way to Britain, so complicated news. Some of my friends recommended a girl who can give you love for just 5 euros. As matter of fact you can deny this because you are in the jungle. Fridays and Saturdays were days for sex and drugs, some of the migrants being slave to their agonies and ecstasies so they gave up the idea of taking their chances to go to the UK.

They just eat, drink, take drugs, even though it was so expensive to buy, but most of those people were forced to buy their own food, I mean oil, flour, sugar, milk and even clothes which they get from the voluntary organisations to get drugs and sex. Therefore, it wasn't unexpected to find thieves and burglaries at night, some of the migrants went away for their chance, others were exhausted so they stayed at their tent chatting and singing, others at the bar dancing and drinking. So it wasn't strange to see a fight start at any time, day or night. I remember one day while I was sleeping I heard someone calling "FIRE. FIRE!" Fortunately I woke up on time, I mean before the fire burned my tent. The next morning I discovered that the fire was intentionally started by a drunken man who had asked the girl for sex and she had refused him but he didn't only burn her tent, he burnt a whole block.

In Ashram kitchen I regularly went there to have tea and coffee and some chat with the friendly people: Henry, Robin and the others. "No coffee , No Chai, like No woman No cry" I still remember them.

# Chapter Twelve

### A SCARY NIGHT

It was seven in the evening when I sneaked on the lucky, scary lorry. My friend opened the back door for me and hugged me for the last time. I felt that warm feeling.

"I wish this will be the last time to see you in France."
"I hope so."
"Don't worry, we will meet again, I know."
"Bye."
"Bye."

I know that he was positive: this time you are going to make it. Before he closed the door he said:

"Don't move and if you have to, just try to do it as quiet as a mouse."

"Ok bye."

The lorry driver was sleeping so I sat there beside the door. It was dark and damp. I walked until I reached the beginning of the stock which was a yoghurt with blueberries. It was too high for me to reach. I tried to reach the top. I failed the first time, but I gathered my strength then I jumped as high as I could. Again I failed. I stopped because I thought that my movement might awake the driver because the whole lorry started to bounce a little.

However, if I stay here the scenario will change so when the driver comes to check the lorry he will find me and he will call the police and I will miss this golden opportunity.

All the journey and tragedies and the hard times that I have been through in just seconds flashed in front of me, though it was dark, I could see these memories obviously. I said to myself "try one more time and this time let those horrible memories be the motive to refuse the fear, corruption, unfair society, loss of my dream job and racism." In a blink of an eye I found myself on the top. I prayed many times. I don't remember how many times but I think as four months in the "jungle".

I tried to find an appropriate place to be hidden as "Tasbina". I did, it was three nail biting hours, I kept praying. At ten o'clock the driver moved in his cabin then he started the engine. He stayed there for five minutes then I heard his footsteps coming to check the lorry. I ceased breathing for two minutes; he opened the door, he was singing "West Virgina". I lowered my head and my body as much as I could so as to not be seen by the driver. I wished I was bald so my hair wouldn't be a reason to be spotted. He checked quickly, and closed it but when he came back again this time carried a torch, a very bright one just like the police's one. He didn't know that what he is afraid of still existed. He closed the door and in myself he opened many wishes and dreams. I raised my head and my body and waved "YES".

After fifteen minutes he commenced moving. I was so delighted, I was on cloud nine. Now I could move my body and breathe freely because I couldn't feel my legs anymore, but something happened which I wasn't prepared for. The driver switched on the freezer and in seconds the temperature dropped to zero and it was so cold. I felt the cool current above my head so I moved my jacket to cover my head or soon I would be unconsciousness.

Forty minutes later he stopped for refuelling and the situation was getting worse but in my inner soul I kept saying "Hold on" so I determined not to move and stay still. Ironically when the lorry arrived at the port or so I thought, because the humps in the street tells you that, because I have been a couple of times – ironically I hoped that anyone would open the hell cold lorry and set me free. I was paralysed in my place, no longer feeling my legs. The lorry stopped and I could feel the tyres sliding on an iron surface – I knew that sound, since I was a child I used to travel by ferry so I knew how it sounds. At first I was thrilled to be on the ferry. I breathed gently until the engine stopped and the freezer also stopped too. Eventually, I felt a slight motion then I heard the most fabulous sounds that I have ever heard in my life so far, the squawk sound of the train. Hoorary, "YES"! I was overjoyed. I took out my mobile and I called my friend. I burst into tears telling him that I had made it to Britain. He congratulated me and advised me not to rush and bang for the driver to stop. "Wait half an hour then after that you can do whatever you wish" and I heard him yelling "Oh, Fellows, Ali has made it" then the linewent dead. I sent a message to my brother "Britain".

I had achieved one of my ultimate goals: to reach England. Then suddenly worries started to run through my soul. The driver, after thirty-seven minutes, switched the engine and freezer to the highest point and after just a few minutes I was cold again, the heat of joy just melted in such a low temperature. I crawled till I was off the stock and on the floor and I hurt my calls I cancelled. , It was half an hour or more, my heart was barely beating, as if it always does at a moment of considerable danger. Was I going to be buried in this freezer lorry? I have never imagined it, all my life I know it, it was the end but I have never thought my grave would be so cold. I thought about my family, how are they going to know about my death and what sorrow they will feel to their loss, between supporting and against the idea of immigration itself. They will feel "R.I.P.", this was his fate, not one can run away to avoid it. I saw them individually how they would react upon news of my death. I banged on the side of the lorry with all my strength, but it was in vain, it didn't work. The excitement turned into horror, fear to die here in this lorry just like other migrants I have lately seen on the TV. I broke out into tears and dialled 999. It was just like the grave, darkness and cold air penetrating my lungs. I was shivering, I couldn't feel my whole body, what a fucking bloody cold!

# Chapter Thirteen

I have heard many stories, horrible ones as well as the luckiest ones about crossing the UK border, individuals who lost their lives in order to try and make it.

'Dingle' I don't mean the nice town in Ireland but I do mean the rear axle's cavity, whether is it hypoid or Planetary rear axles of any lorry or big van or bus; this place is the solo refugee's favourite place for completing their border crossing. On some occasions a border agency official came to visit Salam camp to inform the refugee that there is no difference whether you stay here or you take the dangerous route to reach the UK, if you really have a strong case that grants you asylum, and then gave them some scary stories about dead bodies found in the sea and on the train's track; therefore, for your own safety stay away from the port and trains. Nevertheless, the migrant wouldn't stop trying and obsessing about crossing the border.

Some believe that dingle is a matter of suicide. Faisal spent eighteen days in wintertime at Calais and after he got rid of his cold and bad situation he decided to use dingle and eventually in the blink of an eye he made it. Tesfai, an Eritrean young man in his early twenties, was found dead with a completely crushed skull, and all his brain scattered on the motorway. Osama also made it through the dingle but with some minor injuries on his back from the heat and the movement of the roll drive which he later called it 'a scar of luck'.

In Calais the longer you stay the more you see and hear different strategies and at that time you become more expert among the migrants and you get a full understanding of the migrants' lives and issues. Those who stayed longer atthe camp they have been named 'Makana' or expert and those who arrived late they have been called 'Sarookh' – it means rocket; thus, when those new arrivals make it through the people say 'Fajar' which means the rocket had exploded at his target and reached the UK.A Party will take place celebrating the success of those who cross the border and arrive safely; sometimes you find others like Omar who had a psychological shock when he knew all his friends had crossed – those he himself had helped and locked them in the lorry. He was still saying 'You know what? I locked them, I locked them'.

I am not the good example for the horrible stories because D.J., one of the Sudanese bunch of friends who spent three bloody days with only sips of water and biscuits in a very tiny place underneath a bus ironically, when they arrived in London, they were totally naked, only boxers on them, even the bus driver couldn't believe his eyes – how could six individuals be in such a place, he was so shocked.

Yasir was the bravest one, because he managed to sneak to the port; although the French police were there he hid behind the bus until passengers' passports have been given back to the passengers. He helpedthe driver to put the luggage back into the compartment of the bus and with the last piece he told the driver:

"Leave it, I will do it."

When the bus driver returned to his seat and looked in the side mirror, Yasir had vanished, though he was just there beside the compartment.

Before the driver could investigate what was going on, the police commanded him to approach the ferry. Yasir was inside the bus's compartment hidden behind the bags. Therefore, when he arrived in Dover he directly went to claim asylum at the nearest police station.

You can't tell that Yasir was a migrant! Or illegal refugee, because he was so elegant and so tidy and neat with trendy shiny cap and blue headphones; he always said that the music was the only thing that was keeping him alive.

Mussa'b is the one who only spent two hours in the camp. He got his stuff and drank a bottle of water and one of the migrants advised him to walk with them – maybe you will be the chosen one. He was so worried and scared of the police because he had had a traumatic experience with the Sudanese police. They approached a lorry which was parked beside a petrol station; they told him to sneak in the back door and try not to wake the driver. He was so slim so it was easy for him to do it fast and in a slight way, and with a small knife he cut the canvas on the top of the lorry and got inside. After only forty minutes Muss'b was in Dover claiming asylum and sent his blessing and good wishes to his friends at the west bank of the English Channel.

# Chapter Fourteen

### 999

In fact, I can't remember the exact conversation with the 999 operator; however, I can recall some of it.

"HELLO, what's your emergency, would like police or ambulance?"

"I need them both," I answered. There was silence for a minute then a female voice from the other end:

"What is your name?"

"Ali."

"Where are from, Ali?"

"Sudan"

"Where are you now and why do you need police and ambulance?"

"I am in a freezer lorry."

"Where?"

"In UK."

"Please tell me more! How did you get into the lorry?"

"My friend helped me, I mean he locked me in here."

"From where exactly?"

"France."

"Which way did the lorry take?"

"What do you mean?"

"Was it by ferry or train?"

"By train."

"OK, I can't hear you well. I will pass you to my colleague here, ok. Hold on."

"Hello, my name's Mike, ok Ali, can you tell me a little about you?"

"Ok, my name's Ali, I am from Sudan."

"What is your job in Sudan?"

"I was a teacher."

"Brilliant, you speak very good English."

"Thank you, so help me out of this lorry."

"Ok."

"Hello hello?"

I thought the line was dead then suddenly:

"Hi yeah, I'm here."

"Ok, please help me."

"Ok Ali, don't panic, you said you came from France, is that right?"

"Yes."

"How did you make your way from Sudan to France?"

I knew that the police needed to distract my attention and to keep me focused, many movies I have watched did the same, but I answered him:

"From Sudan to Libya by car through the Sahara and from Libya to Italy by death's boats."

"It was a long journey, wasn't it?"

"Yes it was."

"Do you have a smartphone?"

"No."

"Ok can you try to bang on the side of the lorry!"

"I banged many times but the driver didn't hear me."

"In that case try to find something metal, solid. You can make a noise inside the lorry then the driver will stop."

"You know the whole stock is yoghurt, nothing else."

"Ok can you hang up and call me back so that I can trace your call and find you."

"Ok."

I hung up hesitantly as one minute was a decade for me – I could barely hold the telephone, then the sound beep, beep…

"Hello, what's your emergency?"

"Police please."

"Hello, is that you, Ali?"

"Yes, thank God."

"Are you ok?"

"Shaking and shivering."

"I'm afraid I can't help you."

In this moment I started to feel the bitterness choking me, I couldn't speak, I found the tears poured down my face.

"How?"

"Sorry for that."

"hmmmm-hmmm-hmmm."

"Hi, Ali, are you still there?"

"Yes I'm–"

I no longer could control myself anymore, so I burst into tears and cried like children.

"Don't cry, I'm trying to find you."

"Ok good."

"Could you please tell me what time you arrived in Dover?"

"About 1:30 a.m."

"Great."

I heard him speaking with another police officer in the station and someone on the radio.

"Hey, we are going to find you. Hang up and don't worry."
The hope now vanished.

# Chapter Fifteen

"Al-Moled" is a huge, vivid and full of joy religious celebration which takes place every year according to the Islamic calendar in the third month. I was seven years old when I went on my first experience to the Banat Square where the ceremonies take place. My brothers and sisters were in their new clothes, they were very happy and they kept remembering the last occasion when they did so and so. I was so excited and eager to see this big celebration.

The people gather from different parts of Nayala city so it was so crowded. Many auditions from different games and different magicians and many various activities. When I arrived at the square I was genuinely shocked at the number of people, maybe there were ten thousand – for me they were all the population of Sudan. We went to an old woman not far from the square, maybe she was a relative. We left our stuff there in order not to take many things while we were on the move. It was 5:00 p.m. I mean before the sunset – the view needs an artist to draw this wonderful picture. I was so delighted to see the celebration for the first time. I kept looking around in order not to miss a single moment. My elder brother Ibrahim told me not to let his hand go, "otherwise you will be lost and may be taken away by an evil person, so take care and don't lose my hand" then we dived into the crowd.

An open, well-lit area with loud noises and screams of children on swings and the roller-coaster. I stuck to my brother's hand. I wished I could try the rollercoaster but I wasn't brave enough to do that because I believed that maybe it would lose its balance and run away from the track and people would die immediately. Some sweets were designed and decorated with colourful views so it was to attract the viewer, specially the children. I was looking at one of these dolls when I found myself alone.

First of all I tried not to be afraid because I knew Ibrahim might make fun of me if I seemed afraid, so I stayed calm for minutes then when I realized the danger I started to cry, and cry nobody cares for me. I knew that if I didn't rely on myself I would stay here till morning or worse, be taken by an evil stranger. I decided to leave this crowd so that I could think properly. Suddenly a car appeared out of the dark and by its beam I could recognize the same path we had taken earlier that evening to that old woman, so I went towards the house. It took me ages to reach there. I knocked on the door and the same old woman opened the door for me. I just hugged her, crying. She asked me what was wrong. I told her the whole story, she comforted me and gave me some warm milk and I went to sleep … I banged the door, I banged the door but in vain. I took this inspiration to help me recall the event in France so that the police could save my life. I flashbacked from Calais to Boulogne and how we made it while the police were at the station. We arrived at Boulogne at seven then we headed to the fish company where I found the lorry. OH, My God, I remember the colour of the head of the lorry, it was brown so it was unique colour and there was a sign on each side, Redruth and Cornwall. I forgot the pain and I was lucky to find the mobile still had some charge on it otherwise the police would find me dead inside the lorry. I held onto this faith and dialled 999 again to tell them the features of the lorry but in just minutes the police said we have found you and soon the lorry will stop. At first I doubted it, but soon he was right and suddenly the lorry stopped and I yelled "it stopped". Then the police officer said "welcome to the UK".

A few minutes later a police officer opened the door of the lorry and I found the ambulance was waiting for me. They just took me and put me in their warm car, they told me that "you have Hypothermia, so all you need is to be calm and try to fight shivering". They gave me a bar of chocolate. Meanwhile, the police were checking whether the driver has been convicted of smuggling before or not, the police officer also checked the lorry to see and said laughing it was "just -3 degrees, it is normal, this is the UK".

It was 2 a.m. when the police took me to the station where I claimed asylum and made the fingerprints and had my photo taken. I felt thrilled and waited for 12 hours or so till the immigration officers arrived.

While I was there I said to the police officer, "This cell is a heaven to me because I know that I will be fine and am in a safer place, regardless that it was prison." She kept checking on me from time to time: "Are you OK?" She advised me to have a shower and something to eat.

At five o'clock in the evening the immigration officer arrived and told me they needed to take me to London first to collect some other asylum seekers. The driver was funny, he said, "I wish you are soon granted your status and to be integrated into society – you look like a gentleman." Moreover, when we approached London he started to show me the sights of London and when he finished he asked me for 30 pounds. I asked him why and he said, "I show you the whole of London – do you think that was free?" and laughed. The lady beside him just smiled.

# Chapter Sixteen

SOMEWHERE IN SUDAN

Abdulrahman worked on his land as hard as he could in order to harvest the crops on time before they became wasted by shepherds who let their cattle into the field for better grazing land; therefore, from time to time disputes may occur but thank goodness it is easily resolved through the local authority represented in sheikhs and Omadahs.

Abdu's farm always produces loads of Dura and some other crops like watermelon…etc. The harvested crop could provide sustainable food sources for the whole family and a good amount of money for other household stuff; however, this year Abdu isn't that confident and enthusiastic about it because he used to work with his brother Ali and together they achieved more crops. Abdu hasn't heard any news about him. Ali was the smile that softened the hardship upon his face, Ali had the sense of humour that could erode tiredness and cheer him up when he wanted to, Ali with his charismatic character could influence many friends and willingly work collectively which is known as 'Nafeer' from the early stages of the planting until to load the crops onto the horse carriage to be delivered and stored for the whole year. Now Abdu has to do the all the job by himself, which means he has to work two shifts: one early in the morning lasting for almost five hours ending at eleven o'clock; then after that he returns home for breakfast with his family who are all at school age. He enjoys the coffee and takes a nap till three o'clock then he prepares to go back to the field.

Abdu is a humble man who hardly speaks and approaches other people unless he is asked and requested to do so. Working in the field all his life made him so tough with a steel grip that you feel when you shake hands with him. He has a deep opening or cracks on his feet and sometimes his little son would play with them using a pen to track the narrow cracks' bending. One day he had been stung by a scorpion during his work, though ironically he thought that he might feel a normal numbness on his left foot so he scratched it against a hard dry land, you can imagine the sound consequently when the numbness continued and he discovered that it was a scorpion because he found some remains of it between his foot cracks. He never panicked, just smiled, then picked certain leaves from a plant and started chewing them; the numbness and poison neutralised and he continued his work. Sometimes bad features could be an advantage.

He has such limited knowledge about technology, he never knows how to use the e-mail and Facebook, he hasn't even got a mobile phone and consideredthem a waste of time; therefore, he would prefer to work on the land rather than spending time on the phone. Nevertheless, he is very eager to know any news about Ali, and he usually sits down from seven o'clock in the evening in the youth club to watch the Channel 9 news. One day his neighbour Omran told him that Ali rang him "and he wanted to speak to you".

"My brother Ali! Are you serious? Is he Ali? Sure?"

"Positive," said Omran.

"Where is he?" asked Abdu.

"I have no idea. Soon he will call again and you can ask him."

Moments passed so heavily that from Abdu's perspective it looked like ages, so when the mobile phone rang Abdu answered it on the first beep.

"Hello," Abdu excitedly shouted.

"Hello Abdu, how are you? Miss you, brother!"

"How is your family? I hope they are fit and well."

"Yes we are all fine, how about you tell me do you need any help?"

"Actually I am in Libya and I have decided to travel to Europe. I know it is so dangerous and a matter of live for good or die for good, but it's chaos here in Libya; therefore, it's not safe to stay longer."

"May Allah be with you at all times."

"Thank you. In fact, I would like you to do me a favour, I need some money for this journey."

"Ali, brother, don't worry I can manage that but the question is how will we send you the money?"

Ali explained the whole issue with Abdu, though, it was a human network, mainly from Sudanese and Libyan and other nationalities under the surveillance of the government.

Abdu sold some of his precious cattle to meet the huge amount of money; to be fair, he would never hesitate to help his brother. Money transferred and Ali assured Abdu about his ambition, about the good chance to live a decent life in that part of the world. He asked him to look after Yousef and his mom. Abdu felt worried about Ali's destiny.

In the youth club on his chair Abdu burst into tears

when he watched flipping boats full of migrants who have just drowned in front of the camera. He felt so sorry for them; however, he wished that Ali wouldn't be among the dead.

Next day as his daily routine began he felt different with a broken heart from what had seen yesterday. He went to farm his land but all his thoughts were on Ali. He started working and after two hours he saw on the horizon somebody approaching him on a donkey's back. In the beginning it was only a white colour then gradually appeared to be Omran his friend and he was shouting but Abdu couldn't understand him from far away. He dropped the hoe from his hand and moved towards Omran.

Omran asked for a special gift in return for his package of news. Joyfully, he told Abdu that Ali had just phoned him from Italy and he is safe and sound. Abdu unconsciously hugged Omran and thank him so much for such wonderful news. Omran also asked Abdu to buy a mobile phone, at least the dummy one.

"Omran, my brother. You know I can't deal with technology and mobiles, so could you please buy one for me and sort it out?"

Soon Abdu could know every little thing his brother Ali encountered and lived the miserable situation with him from Italy to France. Meanwhile, Abdu was getting along with his mobile and looked forward to buying a smartphone.

One day a message beep woke him up and he frantically rushed towards the mobile. It was a different number starting with 0044; he opened the text message and saw only one word: 'Britain'.

# Chapter Seventeen

*"God will stand with fair state by victorious even it isn't believer, whereas, he won't stand with those who are believers if they aren't fair"*
Anonymous

If you think you have come across different and difficult stages full of hardship or have been tortured almost to death, you might be wrong because another's story is nothing compared to yours.

It was eight o'clock on 12$^{th}$ of October when I had been dispersal and transferred from Bedford Yarl's Wood detention centre to Birmingham. In the minibus with me were three asylum seekers: Emad from Sudan with his lovely smile and obsession for smoking – therefore, when we arrived at the detention centre and there was a five pound pocket money for the detainee. he preferred to take a packet of cigarettes; the others two were from Kurdistan. The driver said to us, "If you would like to use the toilet this is your last chance because the journey may take up to three hours."

At 10:40 pm I arrived at Birmingham's 5 Stone Road, refugee council, where migrants and asylum seekers were settled for a while. Waiting for procedures Emad asked me if I would accompany him for smoking outside by the gate. I knew nobody in Birmingham while Emad had some friends; he told me his future plan that he would settle with his uncle at Bristol which is not far from here. Later an Indian receptionist asked us to attend a meeting in which he stated everything regarding rules and regulations to be followed starting from early in the morning till the end of the day. He stated also ethics and code of conduct. Next morning I discovered the whole place was run by migrants and refugees. The reception, the canteen and even the cleaning staff were migrants themselves. I felt not away from home because we were all on the same boat. The Somali man guided me to 301, my room, where I found Ahmed, an Iraqi young man from Kirkuk; he was very sensitive and quiet.

There I met Amin, a brutal figure, bad mentally tortured young Sudanese man. I have seen him many times in the canteen, I just say hi. One day I saw him outside in the garden drinking tea. I filled my mug which I had been given besides the stuff, I mean a duvet, a pillow and a sheet.I approached him and sat beside him saying "salaam" he replied "salaam".

"My name is Ali."

Then after two minutes of silence he said, "I am Amin."

"Good to know you, Amin, how are you? Are you ok?"

"Yes, yes ... I am ok."

I didn't try to dig deep in himself, I just stated some major advice for him to survive in this country,

"I don't know how to speak English!"

"Never mind, soon you will be to speak English, just practise and try as hard as you can."

After two weeks he exploded in front of me, I mean he emptied his chest. He started the most bitter story that I have ever heard. He said, "I had better not tell you in case you might be affected by it. Actually, I need someone to share this horrible experience with and because you are so considerate and so kind a man I have decided to tell you."

"Thank you anyway for the compliment."

# Chapter Eighteen

*"Death can be in many different shapes;
the worst is one when you are alive"*
Amin

My name is Amin and I am from Darfur. I didn't get any education in my childhood. I used to herd our goats and cattle, such a primitive area, just all my concerns were with my cattle, how they act and the best place for grazing. Most of the time I enjoy singing and throw the stick up in the air and try to catch it. It was late on a lovely afternoon when it was time to go back to the boundaries of my village after a long day. On the way home I could see two militia cars not far from my house. I ran towards them when I heard my mum screaming.

"Please, for God's sake, stop." Weeping, I approached her and one of the ten soldiers slapped me on the face. I saw my little sister who was only thirteen struggle to fight three soldiers who tore her clothes off and started raping her. She screamed and one after another the five soldiers raped her until she fainted and I couldn't do anything. When I closed my eyes they knocked me with the back of their rifle to open them "to see your little sister having good sex and losing her virginity". Then Mum fell down and one of the soldier said, "She is dead. Poor woman, she didn't wait for her turn," and whispered in my ear.

After this shock, I remained with my little sister. I couldn't look at her, because she reminded me of my weakness not to save her from scandal and save her purity and honour, and the dead body of my mum who had died of a heart attack and scattered cattle. I couldn't know what to do. I couldn't sleep, eat or even be at home or kill myself. You just can't imagine that in my presence they did all that!

I stayed for maybe two weeks then I decided to run away from the whole area as I had known the loss of my father in my early years and my witnessing of my sister being raped and my mother dying. I took every risk, hoping to die but it didn't work, even going four days without food and all of sudden I found myself in Libya – you know I have no career but only as a shepherd. I worked for a year and the treatment of the Libyan man. I used to do anything at any time day and night. Regardless of the weather when I was fed up I was determined to take on the adventure of the sea and I know I might meet my death in its waves and be buried down on the seabed. However, even death refused to take me away. Ironically, when I arrived in France and I fixed to the hope, stuck to what the wishes of another to have a great life on this land, or maybe on English soil, and here I am with a big scar on my life.

Another story was Shadi, a Lebanese accountant who worked with a gulf company.He started his story by saying "Ihave worked for more than four years", therefore, the COE was very satisfied with his work. But actually sometimes he took out money without permission and said to me he "just added them as expenses in the office". When I suddenly discovered that the COE was involved in a big money laundering deals and confronted him with the truth, I asked him to return the money back to the treasury otherwise I would call the police. The man felt the danger and tried to remove me from my job and his way, but actually he couldn't find any mistake to sack me over, or to send me away, so one day after a long day when I went out to get my car, a full speeding car appeared from nowhere trying to crash into me. Miraculously I survived. I knew who was responsible for this incident but I didn't have any support or proof, even when I asked the CCTV man in the parking. He said, "I have no authority." When I called the police and the police asked him what the features of the car were, I asked them to come and check the CCTV. Meanwhile, another private number called me. "Are you still ALIVE?" then the line went dead. So I hadn't much time thinking what to do, I just reached home with the sense that at any minute someone is trying to kill me. I told my wife to be prepared because we were no longer wanted here. She asked me where to? This question I didn't have any answer for it, but we would be safe soon. I ordered an UBER and I used my wife's telephone for the purpose of not tracing me through my cell phone which I had left at home, and rushed to Dubai Airport to take the first flight to Paris.

I couldn't believe that when I arrived atCharles de Gaulle Airport safe with my family, and I told my wife everything about the money laundering and the assassination attempt too. Then, he found his way to enter the UK.

Just like a drama and you are sitting in front of the TV, Mr (M) a very decent old man, he barely speaks, is always with his wife and his only son; they looked they didn't belong here. Soon I introduced myself and tried to be more comfortable to speak to, and after a couple of times he said that he was the Libyan minister of justice. First I was shocked but when told me his situation, he is a very humble man with great knowledge, you can't get bored listening to him. He told me how the transition took place in Libya and how his fellow tried to mend the corruption in every part of the government's body. But other parties would like to control the country and started to kill anyone who stood in their way. On YouTube, he showed me his trial of assassination and always told me we are a lost generation and we are just a sample of elite individuals who have been forced to flee their land; we should be in our countries to help the development and the prosperity of the next generations.

# Chapter Nineteen

In Small Heath, I lived my life, spending my time reading and helping refugees in many aspects of life, what they face and giving them advice for their lives, particularly the best way to integration. I felt human again because I have my own room and other facilities, no lines for the bath or shower; you are free to take a shower whenever you wish. The problem that I faced was the right place to spend more lonely moments and my spare time so without hesitation I chose the library. I went there and registered as a member then no longer felt lonely or isolated, and after two months I looked forward to doing a job because as a matter of fact, I couldn't stay the whole month without going out to the cinema. I would love to go to the gym but for the documentation I wasn't allowed to enrol in the gym due to my status. To kill time I sometimes change the placement of the room, I mean the furniture from here to there, put anything in order, do some vacuuming. One day while I was cleaning my room and the living room and I was in my pyjamas. I needed to put the rubbish out in the bin, and suddenly the door behind me closed…

It was three o'clock in the afternoon, the weather was fine with a cool breeze, nobody at home so I stayed by the doorstep thinking what to do. Should I jump the fence from the neighbour's house? What would they say? Should I call the housing officer? Or should I wait until six o'clock when one of the housemates arrived or showed up? An hour went by then it started to rain. Shit! I ran towards the neighbour next door. I banged on the door and after a while a woman opened the door for me. I told her the story but she said, "Sorry I can't help you." Why was that? I started to feel cold and shivery, then I heard my neighbour was trying to open his door. I shouted:

"Hey, excuse me, could you please help me?!"

He asked what the problem is.

He suggested I come inside and have some tea and dry clothes. I thanked him then he opened the corridorfor meso that I could sneak from the back door by the kitchen. Luckily it wasn't closed. I can't express my gratitude enough to that gentleman.

Thinking about my children worried me, because how could they survive without me? Sometimes I tried to fast some days, I suffered a lot but for them I would do whatever it takes, in order to save some money and send it home. From time to time my wife confirmed that "the kids missed you" and she can't stop lying that "soon you are going to meet and live with your dad again".

I can't even remember how they look, I mean the kids Leila, Yousef and Noor. I hope they are well and safe. Soon I will get the papers. I will apply for family reunion but even the feel for the paper is taking so long, more than seven nail-biting months. I wonder how asylum seekers could survive such a limbo and loneliness, they need to integrate and find some friends.

I participated in many occasions like to be a part of City of Sanctuary, and deliver a testimony in the Houses of

Parliament. It was really an awesome experience.

The characters of my tale now live in different areas in the UK.

Amam is now a kitchen porter in Manchester and he is very content with his job which helps him to contribute sufficient financial support for his family. Yasir's love of music led him to one of the night clubs to be a remarkable disc jockey.

D.J. joined one of the gyms and he is in the shape he had always want to be, a muscle man who the chicks run after; therefore, he got a SIA badge and works in one of the luxurious hotels in Leicester city and he wishes he was there when Leicester football club won the Premier League.

Amin struggled to pass the driving practical test twice; however, he is very determined and passed it at the third time and now he is a friendly bus driver who has been nominated the best employee of the month.

I have found my best destination, the place where I feel relaxed, helpful and encourage those who usually enjoy taking the future leaders towards the better prosperity of the country which reflects upon the citizens and public service. I will stay here in this career for the rest of my life.

A short message from a new number stated that if you are free and would you like to join a singing group, come this Sunday for a rehearsal in the Bond. It was from Sister Margaret and she is the director of St. Chad Sanctuary. A big yes, I replied. On Sunday I went to the Bond following the GPS. I discovered that it was Birmingham Opera Company which every year puts on a production related to the opera stuff. There I met Lizzy who used to work with Care4Calais. The opera was by an Italian composer, soul searching and after two months of rehearsals I could say it from my heart. It was my engagement with the English community and culture. The show has taken place at the Grand Central or the New Street Station at rush hour.

The second time with the company I was contacted to come and help with the interpretation because there were many Sudanese people and an Arabic speaker who can't help them. In order not to be lost in the translation. A wake or Lazarus. It was magnificent to be part of such a production. I found myself in the role of actor when a Sudanese asylum seeker had just dispersed to another city and the director asked my help. I was thrilled to be able to act in front of a huge audience who appreciate this kind of classical music. The third time I was totally an observer, just an interpreter in another triumph for the director. Thus I enjoyed the whole show which lasted for a week and got a five star review in almost every newspaper all over the UK. An entirely fabulous production, Shostakovich, Lady Macbeth of Lady Macbeth of the Mtsensk a Russian composer during the Second World War and the opera had been by the Soviet Union leader.

## RETURN TO CALAIS
## ST PANCRAS INTERNATIONAL

### 6:15 PM

This was my first time to travel out of the UK. I was pleased to see my own family, the refugees. The way to France was full of memories, my feelings were mixed. The place was so busy with European citizens who speak different languages, you could hear French, Dutch, Danish and even Chinese and Korean. I felt lonely and lost, but nevertheless, I am a free man now. I approached the gate to scan my ticket on the pass but it didn't work; a French lady with a short black hair with a lovely smile helped me through. My stuff moved through the checkpoint, I put the coat, a watch, wallet and the belt on a tray and my rucksack on another one. After that, the migration officer who is French looked at the travel document that I have then he asked for the Biometric resident permit. I took my wallet and gave it to him. He looked at the card and to me and said happy journey (bonne voyage) to you, with his heavy French accent.

I looked for a place to sit in but unfortunately I couldn't find any so I went to the Pret a Manger and I bought a salad sandwich and bottle of water and just sat down by the railings. I waited for almost thirty minutes and the announcement of the station for boarding on gate 6 coach 1, a long queue. Most admired my height and complimentary gestures in front of me. Just before the door of the train a French young man in his early twenties welcomed me and checked my ticket and guided me to take my seat 77. Just by the gate I put my rucksack on the luggage rack and just relaxed in the cosy seat by the window. In the past when I took the train, any train, even Eurostar in Brussels or Lille, I just found a way to watch the gatekeeper until he or she moved slightly away from the doors and jumped in. Sometimes I went directly to the w.c. and closed it then the train would leave in a minute or so; it was a victorious feeling to make it. I have been captured by the police and been detained many times but they detain me to live in a hotel in a very comfortable room in Calais – it was a dream to me. A big warm bed instead of the pallet one with many mattresses and blankets . It wasn't cold as it used to be in the jungle. Some of those refugees, all their hopes were for a cosy bed, substantial living resources and security.

At last I saw Ali (me) and Ahmed kept by the police officer in a car. I smiled and they smiled back and I knew that it would be an unstoppable movement. The same faces soon would appear over and over again.

Milton Keynes UK
Ingram Content Group UK Ltd.
UKHW021830250923
429364UK00013B/735